Kamisama Kiss

D1290831

ory & Art by

Julietta Suzuki

CHARACTERS

Nanami Momozono
A high school student who was turned into a kamisama by the tochigami Mikage.
Tomoe
The shinshi who serves Nanami now that she's the new tochigami. Originally a wild fox ayakashi.

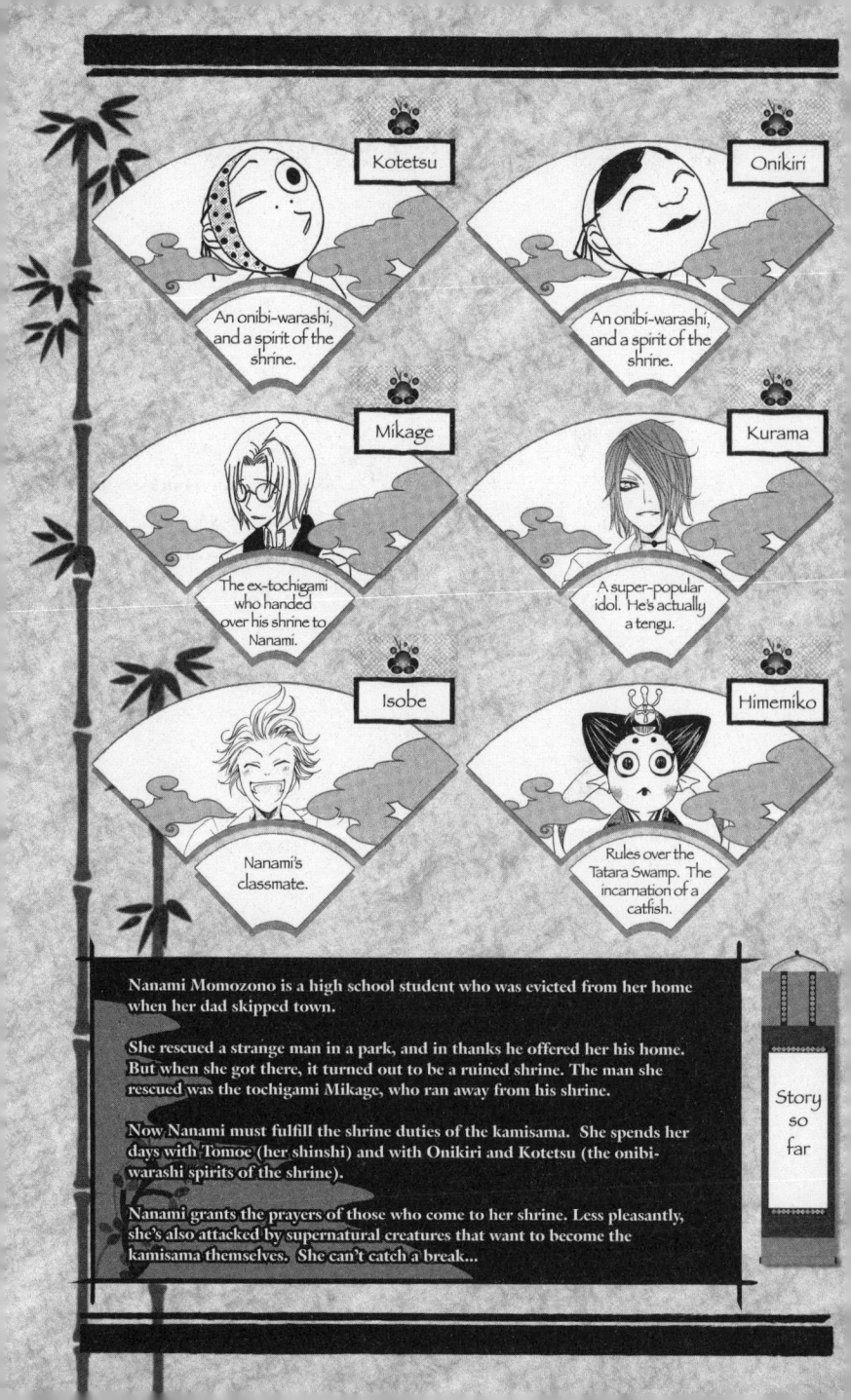

Nanami Momozono is a high school student who was evicted from her home when her dad skipped town.

She rescued a strange man in a park, and in thanks he offered her his home. But when she got there, it turned out to be a ruined shrine. The man she rescued was the tochigami Mikage, who ran away from his shrine.

Now Nanami must fulfill the shrine duties of the kamisama. She spends her days with Tomoe (her shinshi) and with Onikiri and Kotetsu (the onibi-warashi spirits of the shrine).

Nanami grants the prayers of those who come to her shrine. Less pleasantly, she's also attacked by supernatural creatures that want to become the kamisama themselves. She can't catch a break...

Kamisama Kiss

Volume 3
CONTENTS

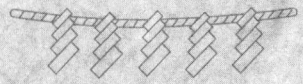

Chapter 13 005
Chapter 14 037
Chapter 15 069
Chapter 16 099
Chapter 17 129
Chapter 18 161
End Notes 191

Kamisama Kiss
Chapter 13

Tomoe's
Ennui Blog
Month O, Day X
I saw a tengu this morning.
Maybe something will happen today.

This is the last page.

In keeping with the original Japanese comic format, this book reads from right to left—so action, sound effects, and word balloons are completely reversed. This preserves the orientation of the original artwork—plus, it's fun! Check out the diagram shown here to get the hang of things, and then turn to the other side of the book to get started!

FLOWER IN A STORM
Story and Art by
SHIGEYOSHI TAKAGI
Riko Kunimi is trying to lead a normal high school life when Ran Tachibana bursts into her classroom demanding that she become his bride. Ran is the richest, most powerful 17-year-old in Japan, and "no" isn't part of his vocabulary. But Riko's got a few superpowered tricks up her sleeve...
A TWO-VOLUME MANGA SERIES
FLOWER IN A STORM
Story and Art by Shigeyoshi Takagi
-1
FLOWER IN A STORM
Story and Art by Shigeyoshi Takagi
-2
Flower in a Storm, Vol. 1
$9.99 USA / $12.99 CAN *
ISBN: 978-1-4215-3241-7
Flower in a Storm, Vol. 2
$9.99 USA / $12.99 CAN *
ISBN: 978-1-4215-3242-4
Shojo Beat
www.shojobeat.com
Manga on sale at store.viz.com
Also available at your local bookstore or comic store
Hana ni Arashi © Shigeyoshi Takagi 2008/HAKUSENSHA, Inc.
* Prices subject to change
RATED T FOR OLDER TEEN
ratings.viz.com
viz media
www.viz.com

FROM THE ANIMATION STUDIO THAT BROUGHT YOU FULLMETAL ALCHEMIST.

SEE THE HOST CLUB
BROUGHT TO LIFE!

TAKE THE BOYS HOME ON DVD
OR BLU-RAY TODAY!

YOU SHOULD BE WATCHING
FUNIMATION.COM/OURAN-HIGH-SCHOOL-HOST-CLUB

Ouran High School

Host Club BOX SET

Story and Art by
Bisco Hatori

Escape to the world of the young, rich and sexy

All 18 volumes in a collector's box with an Ouran High School stationery notepad!

In this screwball romantic comedy, Haruhi, a poor girl at a rich kids' school, is forced to repay an $80,000 debt by working for the school's swankiest, all-male club—as a boy! There she discovers just how wealthy the six members are and how different the rich are from everybody else...

www.viz.com

Ouran Koko Host Club © Bisco Hatori 2002/HAKUSENSHA, Inc.

From the creator of *Ouran High School Host Club!*

Millennium Snow™

By Bisco Hatori

Seventeen-year-old Chiyuki has heart problems, and her doctors say she won't live to see the next snow. Touya is a young vampire who hates blood and refuses to make the traditional partnership with a human, whose life-giving blood would keep them both alive for a thousand years. Can Chiyuki teach Touya to feel a passion for life, even as her own is ending?

Shojo Beat
MANGA from the HEART

Only $8.99

On sale at:
www.shojobeat.com
Also available at your local bookstore and comic store.

Sennen no Yuki © Bisco Hatori 1998/HAKUSENSHA, Inc.

viz media
www.viz.com

You've read the manga, now see the power of a kiss in action!
Kamisama Kiss
FROM THE DIRECTOR OF FRUITS BASKET
BUY IT TODAY!
Get exclusive collectibles in the Goddess Edition including:
• A replica of Nanami's hair stick
• A Tomoe lucky amulet
• A folding fan, tote bag, art postcards and more!
YOU SHOULD BE WATCHING
FUNIMATION.COM/KAMISAMA-KISS
© JS/H·K All Rights Reserved. Licensed to FUN. Produced by TMS.
TMS
FUNIMATION.

KAMISAMA KISS
VOL. 3
Shojo Beat Edition

STORY AND ART BY
Julietta Suzuki

English Translation & Adaptation/Tomo Kimura
Touch-up Art & Lettering/Joanna Estep
Cover Design/Hidemi Dunn
Interior Design/Yukiko Whitley
Editor/Pancha Diaz

KAMISAMA HAJIMEMASHITA by Julietta Suzuki
© Julietta Suzuki 2009
All rights reserved.
First published in Japan in 2009 by HAKUSENSHA, Inc., Tokyo.
English language translation rights arranged with
HAKUSENSHA, Inc., Tokyo.

The stories, characters and incidents mentioned
in this publication are entirely fictional.

No portion of this book may be reproduced or transmitted
in any form or by any means without written permission
from the copyright holders.

Printed in Canada

Published by VIZ Media, LLC
P.O. Box 77010
San Francisco, CA 94107

10 9 8 7 6 5
First printing, June 2011
Fifth printing, March 2014

www.viz.com

www.shojobeat.com

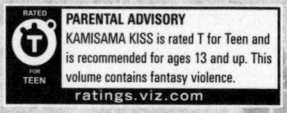

Julietta Suzuki's debut manga *Hoshi ni Naru Hi* (The Day One Becomes a Star) appeared in the 2004 *Hana to Yume Plus*. Her other books include *Akuma to Dolce* (The Devil and Sweets) and *Karakuri Odette*. Born in December in Fukuoka Prefecture, she enjoys having movies play in the background while she works on her manga.

Notes

Page 10, panel 2: Kosode
A basic Japanese robe worn by both women and men, as either an inner or outer garment. The name means "small sleeves."

Page 11, panel 4: Obi
The wrapped sash worn with kimono.

Page 23, sidebar: Takachiho
Many Japanese myths are located in Takachiho, including that of Ninigi, the grandson of the sun goddess Amaterasu, who descended from heaven.

Page 40, panel 3: Tomoe's white too
Many white animals are considered lucky or holy in Japan.

Page 59, panel 2: Day duty, daybook
In Japan, students take turns recording what occurs in the classroom in a daybook.

Page 68, panel 1: PIA magazine
This Japanese magazine specializes in write-ups of culture and entertainment.

Page 75, sidebar: Kendo
Japanese sword fighting. *Kendo* means "way of the sword."

Page 102, panel 4: Went into hiding
A euphemism for dying. This is the expression used when the emperor passes away.

Page 162, panel 1: Softshell turtle
Said to purify the blood and increase stamina (and male virility).

Page 164, panel 2: Kotodama
Literally "word spirit," the spiritual power believed to dwell in words. In Shinto, the words you speak are believed to affect reality.

The Otherworld

Ayakashi **is an archaic term for yokai.**

Kami **are Shinto deities or spirits. The word can be used for a range of creatures, from nature spirits to strong and dangerous gods.**

Kitsunebi **literally means "fox fire" and are the flames controlled by fox spirits.**

Onibi-warashi **are like will-o'-the-wisps.**

Shinshi **are birds, beasts, insects or fish that have a special relationship with a kami.**

Shirohebi **means "white snake" and is a type of yokai.**

Tengu **are a type of yokai. They are sometimes associated with excess pride.**

Honorifics

-chan **is a diminutive most often used with babies, children or teenage girls.**

-dono **roughly means "my lord," although not in the aristocratic sense.**

-himemiko **is a title that means "Imperial princess."**

-kun **is used by persons of superior rank to their juniors. It can sometimes have a familiar connotation.**

-sama **is used with people of much higher rank.**

-san **is a standard honorific similar to Mr., Mrs., Miss or Ms.**

SO I'M ALL RIGHT.

THANKS.

I'M GLAD THIS TOMOE IS WITH ME.

Kamisama Kiss Volume 3 The End

TOMOE'S...
...TENDER HAND.
OKAY.
WHAT'S WRONG ?!
DID MIZUKI DO SOME-THING TO YOU?!
THIS IS THE TOMOE THAT I KNOW.
I JUST ...
...HAD A NIGHT-MARE.
I'M GLAD THIS ONE IS TOMOE...

YOU STILL HAVE A SLIGHT FEVER.
I'LL COOK YOU SOME-THING ...
...SO STAY IN BED.
THIS IS HIS HAND.
O...

WHY ...
HE WAS GOING TO COOK SOFT-SHELL TURTLE SOUP FOR NANAMI-SAMA.
...DID YOU LET THE SNAKE DUDE IN ?!
WHAT DOES THE SOUP HAVE TO DO WITH HIM ?!
NANAMI.
Jolt
HOW'S YOUR FEVER ...?

TOMOE-KUN, WELCOME HOME. HOW WAS SCHOOL?
WHAT'RE YOU DOING HERE?
WAH ...
...IS THAT SNAKE MAN HERE?
HE'S HOME
WHY ...
HSss
HSss
WHAT DID YOU DO TO NANAMI?
GO HOME!
WHAM
HEH HEH.
I'm not telling you! ♡

I SENT YOUR SOUL TO THE PAST.
WHAT YOU SAW WAS A WORLD FROM THE PAST THAT LINKS TO THE PRESENT.
WERE YOU ABLE TO MEET ...
Flinch
...TOMOE-KUN?
NO.
WHO ...
...DID YOU WANT TO MEET?

WELCOME BACK.
YOU WERE AWAY FOR QUITE SOME TIME.
...
THIS IS
Water, water
... YOUR SHRINE.
NANAMI-SAMA!
Wah!
I WAS WORRIED BECAUSE YOU WOULDN'T WAKE UP!
...ASLEEP ?
WAS I ...
MY BODY ...
...FEELS HEAVY.
NO ...

...HE'LL CUT YOUR HEAD OFF WHILE YOU'RE ASLEEP.
SLIP
KYAAAAAH!
I SEE.
THIS MUST BE A DREAM.
NANAMI-CHAN.

NO.
Kssssh
Pant
Pant
NO.
HE WAS A WILD FOX.
NO.
IF YOU DON'T WATCH OUT...

I HEARD THERE WERE BEAUTIES HERE ...
...BUT THE VILLAGE ONLY HAD OLD BAGS AND UGLY WOMEN.
SOME OF THEM GOT AWAY ...
...SO MAYBE THE BEAUTIES MANAGED TO GET AWAY TOO.
SO EVEN THE YOUNG GIRLS RAN AWAY. YOU'VE LOST YOUR EDGE ...
...AKURA-OH.
DID YOU SEE A HUMAN AROUND HERE?
A YOUNG WOMAN NAMED YUKIJI.

WHAM
CHAK
?
TOMOE ...
THIS IS WHERE YOU'VE BEEN LOAFING, BROTHER.
TOMOE.
I WAS TAKING COVER FROM THE RAIN. I DIDN'T WANT TO GET WET.
OH COME NOW.
SOMEONE'S HERE!
I'VE GOT TO RUN AWAY NOW!

WHO ARE YOU?
HMPH.

H...
KYAH!
YOU HAVE A GOOD SET OF LUNGS TOO.
GRAB
HE'S NOT...
NOW CRY FOR ME...
...HUMAN.
HE'S NOT TOMOE.
BITE

TOMOE?
I SEE.
SHE'S A GOOD WOMAN ...
...FOR A HUMAN FROM A SMALL VILLAGE.
NO.

TOMOE.
A VILLAGE GIRL.

FWOOSH
...
K...
...KITSUNEBI
...
SHOOO
T...
GARBAGE ALWAYS BURNS WELL.
TOMOE
...
...SAMA
...
めらめら

...BEFORE AKURA-OH-SAMA FINDS OUT.
HE TAKES AWAY ALL THE GOOD WOMEN.
...
NO!
HE'S A YOKAI...
I'LL EAT YOU ...
SOME-BODY...

I'M GLAD THERE WAS AN ABANDONED HOUSE NEARBY.
IT'S SHABBY, BUT WE CAN GET OUT OF THE RAIN.
WE GOT PRETTY WET ...
SHOW ME YOUR WOUNDS. I'VE GOT TO BANDAGE THEM ...
RIP
THE YOKAI ...
... WOUNDED A CHILD SO SERIOUSLY ...
WOW ...
...I WAS LUCKY.
YOU JUST HAPPENED TO BE AWAY FROM THE VILLAGE WORKING THE FIELDS.
AKURA-OH-SAMA WOULDN'T LET A KNOCKOUT VIRGIN LIKE YOU GET AWAY.

YOKAI ?!
I...
...MANAGED TO RUN AWAY ...
AKURA-OH IS LOOKING FOR YOU ...
...BUT EVERYONE ELSE WAS ...
A YOKAI ...
...IS LOOKING FOR ME ?!
IS THIS ...
...REALLY A DREAM ?!

THIS MUST BE ...
I SEE.
UGH.
...A DREAM ...
IT HURTS ...
A CHILD!
HEY.
UHN ...
WHAT HAP-PENED ?!
DON'T ...
... RETURN TO THE VILLAGE ...
A BUNCH OF YOKAI... ATTACKED US ...

OUCH ...
HEY ...
WHAT DO YOU MEAN ...
...“WHAT TOMOE IS REALLY LIKE”?!
OH?
WHY ARE MY HANDS SO SMALL?
?
pat
pat
pat
?
MY CLOTHES ...
...AND MY HAIR ...
...ARE DIFFERENT.
...IN SOMEONE ELSE'S BODY!
I'M ...
...

GO LOOK...
...INTO THE DISTANT PAST BEFORE YOU WERE BORN.
SEE TOMOE-KUN...
...BEFORE YOU MET HIM ...
FLASH
UGH.

INTO THE PAST, WAY BEFORE YOU WERE BORN.
OH?
YOU'LL SEE ...
...THE TOMOE-KUN YOU DON'T KNOW ...
I'M ...
I'LL HAVE NANAMI-CHAN ...
...PLAY IN THE THRESHOLD OF TIME FOR A LITTLE WHILE.
NANAMI-SAMA ?!
DON'T WORRY.

THEN GO LOOK ...
...AT WHAT TOMOE-KUN IS REALLY LIKE ...
...WITH YOUR OWN EYES.
MIZUKI-DONO!
THAT INCENSE BURNER ...?
YES, THIS ...
...IS THE INCENSE BURNER THAT TURNS TIME.
IT IS A KAMI'S TOOL THAT CARRIES A SOUL INTO THE PAST.
KURAMA
Thank you for letting me draw here!
I love Kurama-kun.
★ Kaga ★

...
HE'S ...
...WON YOU OVER, NANAMI-CHAN.
WELL, THAT'S TOMOE-KUN.
A SHINSHI IS A KAMI'S SERVANT ...
...BUT HE'S TAMED YOU INSTEAD.
IF YOU DON'T WATCH OUT, HE'LL CUT YOUR HEAD OFF WHILE YOU'RE ASLEEP.
N...
NO, TOMOE ISN'T LIKE THAT ...
Sigh
YOU'RE SO STUBBORN, NANAMI-CHAN.
Stubborn ?!

DON'T TALK ABOUT TOMOE ...
...THAT WAY.
I DON'T WANT YOU TO JUDGE HIM...
...BY HIS LOOKS OR HIS BIRTH.
I'M WITH HIM ...
...AND I UNDER-STAND HIM BEST.
I CAN TELL BECAUSE I'VE BEEN WATCHING HIM ...
PEOPLE OFTEN MISUNDER-STAND HIM ...
...BUT HE'S NICE.
...FROM VERY CLOSE BY.

TOMOE-KUN CROSS-DRESSED AND WENT TO SCHOOL ?!
UH HEY!
I'LL PUNCH YOU IF YOU PUT THE TURTLE IN THE POT LIKE THAT!
Oh, no!
YOUR KOTODAMA BINDING IS POWERFUL.
I DIDN'T USE IT.
I ASKED HIM TO GO.
...
YOU ASKED HIM ...
TOMOE-KUN IS PRETENDING TO BE AWFULLY NICE IN FRONT OF YOU.
WHAT DO YOU MEAN?
HE WAS A WILD FOX ...
...SO AS HIS MASTER, YOU MUST CONTROL HIM ...
MIZUKI.

OH?
...WHY'S MIZUKI IN OUR KITCHEN ?!
I HEARD THAT TOMOE-KUN IS AWAY! ★
SO I CAME TO SEE YOU.
THEN THEY ASKED ME TO COOK LUNCH ...
OH NO!
Chomp
MIZUKI-DONO, THE TURTLE HAS BITTEN YOUR FINGER!
HUH ?
OUCH!
...
Get some water!
Wah!
THAT DAY I WAS IN BED...
...AND TOMOE WAS AT SCHOOL IN MY PLACE.
WHAT?!

WE HAVE JUST CAUGHT THIS SOFT-SHELL TURTLE.
IF WE MAKE SOUP OUT OF THIS, NANAMI-SAMA'S COLD WILL GET BETTER.
NANAMI, YOU'RE GONNA EAT A TURTLE?
PEOPLE DON'T USUALLY EAT THIS.
I DON'T KNOW HOW TO BUTCHER TURTLES.
UGH...
SO...

Kamisama Kiss
Chapter 18

...WHEN HE'S NOT AROUND.

Hmph...
THEN ...
...I MUST HAVE TOMOE COME TO SCHOOL AGAIN TOMORROW.
?
Here

Ka-chak
ALL RIGHT.
OH?
WHERE'S THE YOKAI?
DID YOU LET IT GO?
...
WELL, ALL RIGHT ...
...BUT BE CARE-FUL.
I CAN'T ALWAYS BE BY YOUR SIDE ...
...AND PROTECT YOU LIKE THAT FOX DOES ...
...SO DON'T GO LOOKING FOR TROUBLE ...

GIRLS LOCKERS
IT'S ALL RIGHT. JUST GO TO P.E. CLASS.
BUT! MOMO-ZONO ...
SMACK
Gyah! Noooo!
UM... KURAMA ...
WHAT DID I JUST SEE?
Please! Noooo!
POING
WHAM POW
UH ...
Noooo
CRACK
GIRLS LOCKERS
YAH!
LET'S KEEP IT ...
PROM-ISE?
...
...A SECRET.

K-KU-RAMA ...
I TOLD YOU NOT TO ENTER DARK PLACES ...
... NANAMI.
UGH ...
THAT HURT. HE'S MEAN ...
oh!
KURAMA ...
HSs
HSss
HSs
TAKE THAT GIRL AND LEAVE THIS ROOM ...
UGH.

YOU TASTE LIKE STRAW-BERRY.
STRAW-BERRY.
WHAT...
...IS THAT?
KYAAAAAAAH!
2-2
Nekota
ENOUGH.

LICK
YOU DON'T TASTE LIKE ANYTHING.
YOU TASTE TER-RIBLE.
...
I DON'T LIKE YOU.
WAIT ...

I SHOULDN'T BE BOTHERING WITH YOU ...
...BUT I MUST GET RID OF YOU ...
...FOR NANAMI'S SAKE.
WELL WELL.
WHAM
MOMO-ZONO!

I LIKE THIS PLACE.
LOTS OF GIRLS COME HERE AND TAKE THEIR CLOTHES OFF.
I WAS ONLY WATCHING.
I DIDN'T DO ANYTHING WRONG.
SO DON'T BURN ME.
YOU'RE A LECH, A LOW-LIFE.

DASH
K...
KEI!
THERE YOU ARE!
THE TEACHER'S ALREADY IN CLASS.
SHEESH! YOU'RE SO SLOW ...
DID YOU SEE MOMO-ZONO IN THE LOCKER ROOM?
YOU AND MOMOZONO ARE THE ONLY ONES WHO HAVEN'T SHOWED UP.
AMI.
I'LL GO CHECK!
AMI ?
Huh?!
DASH
I...

2-2
Nekota
YOU GO TO CLASS QUICK.
WHAT ABOUT YOU?
I'LL FINISH UP HERE.
Flinch
GO.
YOU'RE IN MY WAY.
...

I WAS LOOKING FOR YOU.
THE GIRL IN CLASS 2.
Glom
MOMOZONO!
WHEN I RETURNED TO THE CLASS-ROOM ...
...NO ONE WAS THERE, SO I WENT LOOKING FOR—
A GHOST!
THERE'S A GHOST!
IT LICKED MY FACE.
I KNOW.
IT'S A GUEST FROM THE OTHER WORLD.

LICK
WHAT DO YOU TASTE LIKE?
TASTES LIKE STRAW-BERRY.
GYAAAAAAAH!
SOME-BODY!
NOO-OOO OO!
SPLAT
Nekota

Whoo
KEI, DON'T TURN THE LIGHTS OFF.
IT'S DARK, AND I CAN'T SEE ANY-THING.
KEI ?
Silence...
...
OH NO...
I'M ALONE.
THIS ROOM IS IN THE BASEMENT, SO NO LIGHT GETS IN WHEN YOU CLOSE THE DOOR.
KEI, HOW COULD YOU ...?!
Quiv Quiv
A CUTE, CUTE GIRL.
THE SWEET, SWEET TASTE OF CANDY.

DARKNESS IS THE ENTRANCE TO THE OTHER WORLD.
THAT TENGU ISN'T JUST A FOOL.
THIS MIASMA ...
AN ENTRANCE HAS OPENED SOMEWHERE.
GIRLS LOCKERS
I PUT IT HERE.
YOU'RE SO SLOW.
WAIT!
AMI.
I CAN'T FIND MY HEAD-BAND.
HURRY UP. CLASS IS STARTING!
I'M GOING NOW.

NANAMI.
DON'T ENTER DARK PLACES ALONE.
I'M BEING SERIOUS NOW.
THE MIASMA IN THIS SCHOOL HAS THICKENED.
MIASMA?
HMM.
MY SHADOW...
...HAS BECOME DARKER THAN BEFORE.

THAT'S WHAT YOU'RE WORRIED ABOUT.
I'M SORRY I DIDN'T UNDER-STAND.
Clasp
BUT IT'S A MIS-UNDER-STANDING.
WHAT I REALLY WANT IS TO HAVE YOU ...
...FALL IN LOVE WITH ME ...
WHAP
I'LL KILL YOU THE NEXT TIME YOU TOUCH ME.
UH HEY... YOU HIT MY FACE ...

Tmp
Tmp
WHAT'S WRONG? YOU SEEM TICKED OFF TODAY.
...
IF YOU'RE HAVING PROBLEMS, JUST TELL ME.
I'LL TELL YOU ONE THING.
YOU'RE IN MY WAY. DON'T FOLLOW ME.
HUH?
...
YOU WANT MY HEART, DON'T YOU?
I KNOW YOU WANT TO BECOME A KAMI ...
...BUT IT'S NO USE TRYING.
OH DEAR.

Ooh!
KURAMA'S SINGING IN FRONT OF ME!
HOW COOL!
I CAN DIE HAPPY NOW!
Kyah!
HMPH.
DID I CHARM YOU, NANAMI?
Peek
GLARE
NANAMI.
Bing Bong
FWOOSH
KURAMA
?
?
?

BaFle
MOMO-ZONO.
YOU'RE THE ONLY ONE WHO'S OUT OF TUNE.
SING IT ONE MORE TIME.
MMM, NO.
THE LAST NOTE IS HIGH BY A HALF-TONE.
LET'S HAVE A PROFESSIONAL SING AS AN EXAMPLE!

Peek
HOW WAS THAT, NANAMI?
Ooh!
HE'S WONDERFUL.
KURAMA'S PRONUNCIATION IS PERFECT.
Kyah!
...
Hss
Hss
ALL RIGHT.
STOP!
MUSIC ROOM
Second period
Bing
Bong
Oh?

Baffle
English II
English II
...
English.
WHAT, RE THESE CHARAC-TERS?
WHAT'S WRONG, MOMO-ZONO?
...
START READING.
Teacher.
I'll read instead.
Nanami can't speak in a loud voice because she was sick.
...HAVE TO MAKE MY MOVE.
NEXT PAGE.
START READING AT "BECAUSE" ...
...MOMO-ZONO.

I got a sidebar to draw. ★ Thank you ♡
Shun ★
ARE YOU SERIOUS ?!
HERE'S A COPY OF THE NOTES WE TOOK IN JAPANESE CLASS.
KURAMA
KURAMA
To Kurama
BUT I THINK KURAMA IS MORE HAND-SOME ...
CRAP... THINGS HAVE CHANGED WHILE I WAS AWAY AT WORK.
I WAS GOING TO GET CLOSE TO NANAMI WHILE THE FOX WASN'T AROUND ...
...SO I

Smirk
YOU STUPID TENGU.
...BECOME FEMININE ...
...WHILE I WAS AWAY.
Your clothes
Bing Bong
MY TRANSFORMATION SPELL IS PERFECT.
SCHOOL IS A BREEZE...
WHAT ?!
TOMOE HAS TRANS-FERRED HERE?!
SHOCK
YEAH.
THE GIRLS WERE MAKING A REAL FUSS.
TODAY HE'S OUT SICK THOUGH.
KURAMA

I'VE BEEN AWAY FOR A WEEK.
キャーキャー
キャーキャー
IT'S BEEN A WHILE, NANAMI.
Gah!
TENGU!
キャーキャー
キャーキャー
HERE ARE SOME SOUVENIRS FROM WORK.
KURAMA, THE SUPER-BUSY SUPER IDOL HAS COME TO SCHOOL.
HMM?
YOU'VE ...

W-WHAT IS THAT AURA?
HAS SHE ALWAYS BEEN LIKE THAT?!
Whoa!
I CAN SEE FLOWERS IN THE BACK-GROUND!
HER BOOBS SEEM BIGGER TOO.
NANAMI MOMO-ZONO?!
Grr
Nana-mi.
I'll make you pay for this ...
GOOD MORN-ING.
Tmp

EXCUSE ME ...
...BUT THAT'S MY SEAT.
WILL YOU MOVE ?
N...
N...

Bully
Bully
I SENSE SOMEONE WHO'S GETTING HELD BACK!
MOMO-ZONO'S TAKING TODAY OFF TOO.
SO WHO WANTS TO BET THAT MOMOZONO'S CUTTING CLASS? THE BETS START AT 300 YEN!
ISOBE... YOU SEEM REAL HAPPY WHEN YOU TALK ABOUT MOMOZONO.
...I WON'T BE THE HEROINE OF TODAY'S STORY.
Bing Bong
Tmp
DO YOU ACTUALLY LIKE HER?
OH PLEASE.
MOMO-ZONO BRINGS PLAIN RICE FOR LUNCH.
YOU CAN ONLY MAKE FUN OF–
HEY.

Sheesh
YOU'RE SAYING THAT CUZ IT'S NOT YOUR PROBLEM.
...WHAT IF TOMOE-DONO TRANSFORMS HIMSELF INTO NANAMI-SAMA ...
THEN ...
...AND ATTENDS SCHOOL FOR YOU?
And so ...
WHAT A GREAT IDEA!

YOU'RE FEVER-ISH.

I CAN'T LET YOU GO TO SCHOOL.

THIS IS A GOOD OPPOR-TUNITY.

DON'T ATTEND SCHOOL FOR A WHILE.

Sway
HEY, ONIBI.
DO YOU HAVE ANY COLD MEDICINE?
flushed
I SEEM TO HAVE A FEVER ...
Good morning. I'm Nanami Momozono.
Beep
103.6°F
103.6 DEGREES.
...I'm not feeling well today.
...but because of all the troubles I've had lately ...
Oh no Nanami-sama!
Wah!
Dazed
Being healthy is my one redeeming quality ...
Tromp
Tromp
Tromp

Tomoe's Ennui Blog

Month △, Day ○

Mizuki, a fellow shinshi, came to visit the shrine.

We had tea and talked about the hard life of a shinshi. It was a fun day, and I hadn't had that in a while.

Nowadays, I don't see Nanami much.

Kamisama Kiss
Chapter 17

LET'S GO HOME.
SO SHE DOESN'T BREAK....
SO I DON'T DESTROY HER...

WON'T SHE DIE IF SHE FALLS FROM A TREE?
TOMOE.
YOU'RE NOT ACTING LIKE YOURSELF.
SHE'S SO FRAIL.
IF YOU SAY SOMETHING NORMAL ...
A LIVING BEING LIKE THIS...
...I'LL BE SO HAPPY THAT I'LL DEPEND ON YOU MORE ...
...IS MY KAMI.
HEY ...
...
...
OH, DEAR.
SHE'S TOO MUCH FOR ME TO HANDLE ...

I JUST FELL.
I'M ALL RIGHT.
...
I'M SORRY.
I SHOULD'VE KEPT WATCH OVER YOU...
IF SHE FALLS, SHE BLEEDS.

I THOUGHT ABOUT ...
DON'T WORRY.
...
...WHAT WOULD HAPPEN IF I DIED ...
...AND YOU BECAME LIKE MIZUKI.
YOU HURT YOUR-SELF.
THEN I COULDN'T LEAVE HIM ALONE ...

TOMOE, WHY DO YOU LOOK SO CRANKY?
Tmp
Tmp
IT'S NOTHING.
Grr
YOU ARE ANGRY.
BUT I COULDN'T LEAVE HIM ALONE.
YOU GOT AWFULLY FRIENDLY WITH THAT SNAKE.
YOU PROMISED TO SEE HIM AGAIN RIGHT IN FRONT OF MY EYES.
AM I A FOOL?

I'M SORRY I CAN'T STAY WITH YOU.
BUT ...
...I PROM-ISE.
...WHEN YOU'RE LONELY ...
...I'LL COME LOOK AT THE PLUM TREE AGAIN.
I PROM-ISE.

ENOUGH.
MIZUKI.
TOMOE CAME TO GET ME ...
...SO I'M GOING HOME.

NO!
THAT PLUM TREE IS YONOMORI-SAMA'S FAVORITE TREE.
LET US LIVE HERE FOREVER AND WATCH THE PLUM BLOSSOMS.
FOREVER.
TOMOE ....

YES.
I UNDER-STAND.
I REALLY DO...
TOMOE...
SO ...
...I'LL FORGIVE YOU ...
HSSSSSS
...BY TURNING THAT TREE INTO CINDERS.

I SEE.
YOU LIVE FOR THAT TREE.
EVERY-THING, INCLUD-ING THIS SHRINE ...
...WAS SIMPLY TO DECORATE THAT TREE.
Y...
YOU'RE RIGHT.
THIS IS THE ONLY THING THAT'S LEFT.
YONO-MORI-SAMA'S TREE ...
MY DEAR PRECIOUS TREASURE.
YOU MUST UNDER-STAND.
SINCE YOU ...
...ARE A SHINSHI TOO!

MIZUKI.
I WILL NOT DIE.
I AM ONLY RETURNING TO NATURE.
BUT...
VOW BY THIS PLUM TREE...
...I AM WORRIED ABOUT YOU.
...THAT YOU WILL NOT CRY ALONE ...
I'M GLAD ...
...THE TREE IS SAFE ...
...AFTER I AM NO MORE.

FWOOSH
TWO. I TOOK YOUR HOSTAGE.
ANOTHER LOSS FOR YOU.
THREE, AND THIS LOSS IS FATAL.
MIZUKI-DONO.
MIZUKI-DONO.
THE GARDEN IS BURNING ...

FWOOSH
THE SHRINE.
MY SHRINE ...
PUT OUT THE FLAMES!
...IS BURNING!
TOO LATE.
MY KITSUNEBI HAS ALREADY SURROUNDED THE ENTIRE SHRINE.
ONE. YOU LOST BECAUSE YOU LET ME IN.

THE SHRINE OF A WATER KAMI!?
THAT'S WHAT THIS PLACE IS?
BOTH YOUR WATER KAMI AND HER SHRINE HAVE ROTTED AWAY.
THIS IS A DIMENSION YOU CREATED SO YOU COULD PLAY SHINSHI.
THAT'S WHY I HAD SUCH A HARD TIME FINDING THIS PLACE.
NOW, YOU EX-SACRED SHINSHI ...
...IT'S TIME TO BE PUNISHED FOR MAKING ADVANCES ON MY MASTER!

WELL ...
...YOU USED TO BE A WILD FOX.
Isn't that right?
YOU DON'T ...
...REALLY INTEND TO FIGHT ME, DO YOU?
HOW COULD YOU BE SO DIS-RESPECT-FUL ...
YOU WERE BORN AN AYAKASHI. I AM A SACRED SHINSHI.
...AS TO TRY TO BURN THE SHRINE OF A WATER KAMI?
WE ...
...SHOULDN'T EVEN BE TALKING TO EACH OTHER.
SHINSHI SOCIETY IS A CLASS-BASED SOCIETY TOO?

...
YOU'RE LATE ...
...TO FORGIVE HIM.
OH DEAR.
I NEVER THOUGHT YOU'D FIND THIS PLACE.
SHUU
AND YOU STILL DON'T KNOW HOW TO BEHAVE, TOMOE-KUN.
THE FLAMES!

I'M SO GLAD YOU'RE OKAY...
...THAT ONLY I CAN HEAR.
A HOARSE VOICE.
A SOFT VOICE...
THAT'S ALL I NEED...

TOMOE!
BAM
GET AWAY FROM HIM.
...
...
NANAMI!

DASH
HOW DARE YOU MAKE ADVANCES ON MY MASTER ?!
I HOPE YOU'RE PREPARED TO BE SERIOUSLY PUNISHED.

...TOMOE!
TMP

AM I NOT GOOD ENOUGH FOR YOU?
HYA AH!
KICK
HEY!
YOU SAID YOU WOULDN'T DO ANY-THING!
LEMME GO!
SORRY.
I'VE CHANGED MY MIND.
HEY.
NO!
HELP ME ...

STOVE
I'M SORRY.
I CAN'T STAY HERE FOREVER.
THERE ARE PEOPLE WAITING FOR ME.
TOMOE MUST BE LOOKING FOR ME.
I... HAVE TO GO HOME ...
WHY?

ARE YOU COMFORTING ME?
YOU'RE SO NICE, NANAMI-SAN.
BE NICE ...
...AND STAY WITH ME FOREVER.
LET US LIVE HERE FOREVER ...
...AND WATCH THE PLUM BLOSSOMS.
FOREVER ...

Four

I haven't talked about the manga at all. I wonder if that's all right?

I always wonder whether the readers prefer to read about my daily life or about my manga. I'll be happy if you enjoy both. Well then! I hope we'll be able to meet again.

★ If you have comments or opinions, please send them to the following address

★

Julietta Suzuki
c/o Shojo Beat
P.O. Box 11010
San Francisco, CA
94101

...LONELY ALL THIS TIME ...
...MIZUKI.
UM ...
I'M ...
...A KAMI-SAMA ...
...AND I HAVE A SHINSHI CALLED TOMOE ...
IF TOMOE ...
... WAS LONELY LIKE YOU ...
...IT WOULD BREAK MY HEART.

BUT I WILL STAY HERE.
EVEN IF YONOMORI-SAMA IS NO MORE ...
...I WILL KEEP PROTECTING YONOMORI-SAMA AND THIS SHRINE.
THAT IS MY DUTY AS SHINSHI.
YOU'RE SERVING A MASTER WHO WILL NEVER RETURN ...
...ALL ALONE IN THIS SHELL OF A SHRINE.
THAT IS...
...SO ...
YOU WERE ...

LONG, LONG AGO ...
...THERE WAS A BIG RIVER NEARBY ...
...AND CHILDREN OFTEN DIED THERE.
THE VILLAGERS THOUGHT IT WAS A CURSE ...
...AND BUILT A SHRINE. THAT'S HOW THIS PLACE BEGAN.
A KAMI LIKE YONOMORI-SAMA WHO IS BORN BECAUSE PEOPLE NEED HER CANNOT CONTINUE TO EXIST WITHOUT HER BELIEVERS.
WHEN PEOPLE ABANDONED THIS LAND ...
... YONOMORI-SAMA WENT INTO HIDING.

SO A SHRINE OF A WATER KAMI IS SUBMERGED IN WATER. HOW ABSURD.
TOMOE-DONO.
NANAMI-SAMA IS UNDERNEATH THE WATER?!
DON'T YOU THINK IT WAS PRETTY OLD FASHIONED OF THAT SNAKE TO PUT A BETROTHAL MARK ON NANAMI?
THERE ARE MANY WHITE SNAKES ...
...BUT THERE'S ONLY ONE SNAKE ...
...WHO GREW UP SO SHELTERED ...
...HE'D BE STUPID ENOUGH TO WANT TO MARRY A KAMI.
I'VE FOUND YOU.

TOMOE-SAMA.

WE HAVE FOUND IT.

THE VILLAGE YOU ARE LOOKING FOR IS AT THE BOTTOM OF THIS—

RESER-VOIR.

THERE MUST BE NO HUMANS OR KAMI LEFT HERE.

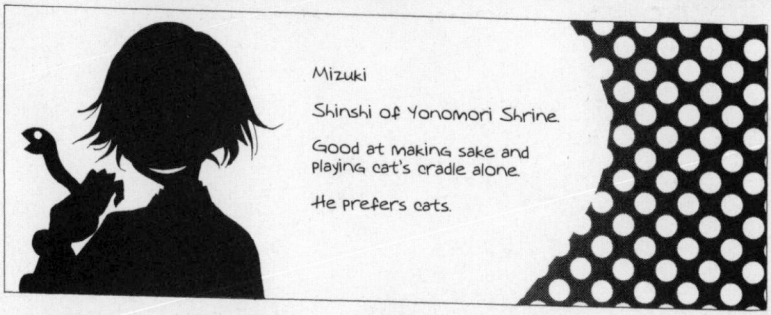

Kamisama Kiss
Chapter 16

AH...
WILL YOU EXPLAIN ...
...WHAT'S GOING ON?
...SO THIS SHRINE...
...DOESN'T HAVE A KAMI.

Tmp
Tmp
I WONDER WHEN IT WAS ...
Um...
UH ...
HEY.
WAIT.
DO NOT TOUCH YONOMORI-SAMA.
TWIP

THERE'S SOMETHING MISSING IN THIS SHRINE.
HUH ?
YOU MENTIONED NO ONE VISITS THIS SHRINE ...
WHEN DID PEOPLE STOP COMING?
MIZUKI.

He's a lowborn white fox.
Yes.
I DON'T WANT YOU GUYS SAYING THAT!
Heh heh
BUT POOR TOMOE.
I CAN SEE HIM SITTING ON THE PORCH ...
...LOOKING DEPRESSED BECAUSE HE'S LOST HIS MASTER ONCE MORE.
HMPH.
YOU'RE THE ONE WHO WAS SITTING ON THE PORCH LOOKING DEPRESSED.

TOMOE IS ...
AND THE SPIRITS OF MY SHRINE BEHAVE.
UNLIKE YOU GUYS.
BOOO
...A GREAT COOK.
HMM.
SO HE'S A GOOD COOK.
YOU KNOW TOMOE?
I DO.
I'VE KNOWN HIM MUCH LONGER THAN YOU HAVE.

NOW EAT IT, HUMAN KAMI!
HERE'S YOUR BREAK-FAST.
HURL
HOW CAN I EAT THIS?!
HA HA HA.
TAKING CARE OF A HUMAN IS HARD.
WAH!
YONO-MORI-SAMA ONLY DRINKS SAKE.
THAT IS WHY THE SAKE MIZUKI-DONO MAKES IS THE BEST IN THIS WORLD.
YONOMORI-SAMA SAID MIZUKI-DONO IS THE NUMBER ONE SHINSHI IN JAPAN.
Glance
Squeak

...SOMETHING IS MISSING.

MIZUKI?

I WILL GET HER BACK ...
...FOR SURE.
WHILE MY HAND CAN STILL REACH YOU...
Ladies' room

WITH HER LIMITED PHYSICAL AND MENTAL ABILITIES, SHE WON'T BE ABLE TO PROTECT HERSELF.
I NEVER THOUGHT I WOULD PANIC LIKE THIS.
SHE MIGHT BE CRYING NOW ...
WHAT SLIPPED FROM MY FINGERS...

TOMOE-DONO IS SO CALM.
HE'S BEEN POLISHING BOTTLES ON THE PORCH ...
...EVER SINCE HE RETURNED.
HE IS THE NUMBER ONE SHINSHI IN JAPAN.
HE LOOKS ABSOLUTELY SERENE.
HE IS SO DEPEND-ABLE.
He must have a plan.
Oops
Crash!
slip
OH NO!
THIS IS THE END OF THE SHRINE!
SHUT UP, ONIBI!

...COME RESCUE ME QUICK ...
NANAMI-SAMA HAS BEEN KIDNAPPED!
NANAMI-SAMA HAS BECOME A SNAKE'S BRIDE!
DO NOT CRY, ONIKIRI.
THIS IS THE END OF THE SHRINE.
WE STILL HAVE HOPE.
Wah!
LOOK.

JUST STAY HERE WITH ME.
Woo!
Woo!
...
FWOMP
SIGH ...
TOMOE ...
I'M HERE.
IF YOU'RE MY SHINSHI ...

THIS ISN'T THE SEASON FOR PLUM BLOSSOMS ...
...BUT THEY'RE BLOOMING.
WE'RE NOT IN THE HUMAN WORLD.
NO.
THAT PLUM TREE IS ALWAYS IN BLOOM.
I STOPPED TIME ...
...WHEN THE TREE WAS AT ITS MOST BEAUTIFUL ...
...BECAUSE IT IS YONOMORI-SAMA'S FAVORITE TREE.
...
YOU WANNA GO TO BED?
I!
I WON'T MARRY YOU!
I WON'T DO ANYTHING ...
...UNTIL YOU WANT TO.

YOU LIAR.
I WANT TO GO HOME...
DON'T CRY.
JUST STAY WITH ME FOREVER.
YONO-MORI-SAMA APPROVES OF IT TOO.
I'LL TAKE MUCH BETTER CARE OF YOU ...
...THAN TOMOE-KUN.

DID YOU FALL?
YOU'RE HURT.
YOU'RE BLEEDING.
WE MUST TREAT THE WOUND.
DON'T MOVE.
I WILL NOT...
...LET ANYONE TOUCH YOU.

Here's a lantern!
...YOU CAN TRY AGAIN.
IF YOU'RE NOT SATISFIED ...
I SAID YOU WOULDN'T BE ABLE TO GO HOME.
...WALKED SO FAR.
BUT I ...
WHY AM I HERE?
Thump
OH?
...HATE THIS GUY ...
I...
NO ONE COMES HERE.
IT'S NO USE WAITING FOR PEDESTRIANS.

LIGHTS.
HOUSES!
THERE ARE PEOPLE THERE!
THERE ARE PEOPLE ...
WELCOME BACK, NANAMI-SAN.
THIS IS THE YONOMORI SHRINE ...

I CAN'T STUMBLE.
I GOTTA WALK.
I REALLY ...
Damnit
I'LL GO HOME!
I WILL GO HOME!
Hya Ha Ha Ha Ha Ha!
...
Clench
IF I WALK JUST A LITTLE BIT MORE.
JUST A LITTLE FARTHER.
Crnch
I'LL...
Crnch
AH.
...WANT TO GO BACK TO MY SHRINE.
I'LL COME HOME.

...BUT THIS IS A PAVED PATH.
IF I WALK ALONG IT, I'LL HIT A HIGHWAY.
FOR SURE.
FOR SURE....
Trip
Klomp
IT'S BEEN SEVERAL HOURS NOW.
UGH.
IT'S JUST THIS PATH, NO MATTER HOW FAR I WALK ...
THERE ARE NO CARS OR HOUSES ...

WHAT'S WITH THESE GUYS?!
I...
I'M GOING HOME FOR SURE.
THEY CAN'T TREAT ME LIKE A FOOL JUST BECAUSE I'M A GIRL.
...CAN LEAVE THIS SHRINE. NO PROBLEM!
SEE?
DASH
EASY!
I LEFT THE SHRINE.
ALL RIGHT.
I DON'T KNOW WHERE I AM ...
But I'm still in Japan.

Argg!
OH, BUT THE MARK ON YOUR WRIST IS OUR ENGAGEMENT RING.
I'M LEAVING, I'M LEAVING!
I WON'T MARRY YOU!
I'M GOING HOME!
I DIDN'T ASK TO BE BROUGHT HERE.
HMM ...
WHY DON'T YOU TRY IT?
Heh Heh Heh
Hee Hee
SEE IF YOU CAN REALLY GO HOME.
Hee Hee
WHA ...?

I DIDN'T REALIZE.
THE KAMI-SAMA?
...IS YONOMORI-SAMA, THE KAMI OF THIS SHRINE.
YONOMORI-SAMA IS CONGRATULATING ME ON MY WEDDING TOO.
NOW, NANAMI-SAN... ♡
NO.

Three

The other day, the magazine Kikan S-sama printed my interview as part of their mythology special. I talked a lot about the manga, so I'd be happy if you read it. This was my first interview, and I was very nervous. Thank you so much!

I've been writing a blog for a couple years, but the other day it was shut down. Uh, I lost it. So I'm telling everyone here. Thanks to everyone who used to read it!

I bought a new pinky ring. I wore my old one for about five, six years. I guess I'll be wearing this one for five, six years too.

Speaking of fingers—because of the way I hold my pencil, I haven't gotten a writer's callous, but I finally have one on my little finger. Because the callous is on my little finger, it really stands out and I feel depressed... Won't this go away? I think I'll put a bandaid around my little finger next time I draw.

When I was in high school, I used to do kendo, and the callous that formed then is still on the sole of my foot... I guess it's not gonna go away... (depressed)

YOU'RE ...
GYAH!
GOOD MORNING, NANAMI-SAN.
I SAW HIM AT SCHOOL ...
THANK YOU FOR RESCUING ME AT SCHOOL THE OTHER DAY.
I AM MIZUKI, SHINSHI OF THIS SHRINE.
WE SHALL BE TOGETHER FOREVER.

IS SHE AWAKE?
NOT YET.
WHERE ARE YOU?!
MMM...
OHO.
SHE'S FINALLY AWAKE.
SNAP
HEY, HUMAN.
YOU WANNA EAT A CENTIPEDE?

Look for Nanami!
FOOSH
WHEN I FIND THAT WHITE SNAKE DUDE ...
NOOOOO!
...I'LL CHOP HIM UP AND MAKE HIM INTO SASHIMI.
NANAMI.

NANAMI.
Kitsunebi!
FWOOSH
WE'RE HAVING TEA AT THE RESTAURANT IN FRONT OF THE TRAIN STATION. IF YOU'D LIKE TO—
ARE YOU LEAV-ING?
Tmp
MIKAGE.
AH.
FOUND YOU.
swarm swarm

Ami Nekota
A female student in Year 2, Class 2.
She drinks milk every morning, but she's stopped growing.
She puts sugar in soy-flavored omelets.

Kamisama Kiss
Chapter 15

YONOMORI-SAMA, LOOK.
THE PLUM TREE IS BEGINNING TO BLOSSOM.
Chapter 15
MIZUKI.
DON'T YOU HAVE A WOMAN TO GO FLOWER-VIEWING WITH?
OF COURSE NOT.
WHEN YOU DO...
...TELL ME RIGHT AWAY.

What should we do today?
FWIP
PIA
Do you want to go some-place?
A DATE
I WOULD LOVE TO GO TO THE BOTTOM OF THE SWAMP.
I WANT TO DRIFT AT THE BOTTOM OF THE SWAMP, JUST KOTARO AND ME.
I cannot tell him that...
AH HA HA HA

A DATE
Wha—!
Ko-taro.
Do you like me?
th-thump
th-thump
I...
...I...
...I...
SHE JUMPS ON HIM
HURL
If you like me!
If you like me!
I DON'T.

SNAP
NANAMI?

THINGS WERE FUN
...
...AND I WAS SO HAPPY
...
...THAT I HAD COMPLETELY FORGOTTEN
...
...ABOUT IT.
NICE WEATHER.

NANAMI.
HELLO.

...
I GUESS HE'S WORN OUT...
I'LL HAVE HIM REST WELL TONIGHT.
AND, I HOPE HE'LL COME WITH ME TO SCHOOL...
...TOMORROW, THE DAY AFTER TOMORROW, FOREVER.

...MUCH MORE ...
I FEEL CLOSE TO TOMOE.
...THAN WHEN WE'RE AT THE SHRINE.
5th period
6th period
SCIENCE
Everyone was very too.
from the teacher...
THERE.
CLATTER
SORRY TO KEEP YOU WAITING, TOMOE.
LET'S GO TO THE FACULTY LOUNGE.
WHAP
I'M DONE WITH THE DAY DUTY.

WE'VE BEEN LIVING IN THE SAME HOUSE ...
TO OBTAIN THE VALUE OF X ...
... APPLY THIS FOR-MULA AND ...
...BUT I DON'T THINK WE'VE BEEN THIS TOGETHER BEFORE.

Tmp
Tmp
Tmp
THIS IS ODD.

YOU'RE ON DAY DUTY TODAY MOMO-ZONO ...
...SO HERE'S THE DAYBOOK.
HERE YOU GO.
?
THANKS ...
Wave
GOOD LUCK.
SEE YOU.
D...
DID SHE OVER-HEAR US?
ARE YOU FRIENDS WITH HER?
TODAY'S THE FIRST TIME I'VE SPOKEN TO HER.

YOU NEED TO GO TO THE BATH-ROOM?
GRAAH!
NO!
IF YOU SAY SUCH THINGS, I...
SHEESH.
DON'T SAY THINGS LIKE "MASTER" AND "SERVANT." PEOPLE WILL MIS-UNDERSTAND.
THEY'LL CALL ME WEIRD NICK-NAMES AGAIN...
SOME-THING WRONG?
SER-VANT ...
ALL RIGHT!
LET'S TELL PEOPLE YOU'RE THE SON OF THE FAMILY THAT ADOPTED ME...
Tmp

THEY'RE THE NAMES OF THE HUMANS WHO'RE TAKING CARE OF NANAMI ...
...SO OF COURSE I RE-MEM-BER.
WH-WHAT'S YOUR RELATION-SHIP WITH HER?
We're not taking care of her.
NANAMI IS MY MASTER—
WAH!
Zoom
NO FAIR! IF YOU ...

...HE WOULDN'T ...
NO...
It's been a while.
Do you remember us?
...FLIRTING AGAIN ...
I DO.
I REMEMBER THE FACES AND NAMES OF EVERYONE IN THIS CLASS.
CHIE KITAMI.
NATSUKO UMIBE.
MEGUMI TOBITA.

Hey Hey!
THE GIRLS, I MEAN.
WHEN KURAMA'S NOT ATTENDING SCHOOL, THINGS ARE QUIET.
HE SEEMS BUSY WITH WORK THIS WEEK.
NO, THEY'RE MAKING A FUSS ...
Chatter
You're Tomoe.
Chatter
You look so different now!
You came to the classroom once to deliver a lunch box.
HE'S...

NOW MOMO-ZONO.
SHARE YOUR TEXTBOOKS WITH TOMOE.
th-thump
THE WAY THINGS ARE TURNING OUT...
...I FEEL LIKE ...
...THANKING THE SNAKE.
THE TENGU IS TAKING THE DAY OFF.

TOMOE IS ALL TENSE ...
...BUT I'M A LITTLE HAPPY ABOUT THIS...
THIS IS TOMOE MIKAGE.
HE TRANS-FERRED FROM MOUNT MIKAGE.
I THINK.
Beverly Hills High School Diaries
I WILL SIT NEXT TO NANAMI.
WHAAAAT.
YEAH YEAH.

WELL... I'M NOT SCARED OF SNAKES ...
WHAT-EVER ...
LAST NIGHT I READ THIS BOOK MANY TIMES.
TH-THAT'S MY FAVORITE BOOK!
Beverly Hills High School Diaries
C-CAN YOU REALLY ACT LIKE A HIGH SCHOOL STUDENT, TOMOE?
I CAN.
YOU DO KEEP CAUSING TROUBLES FOR ME ...
GROUSE
GROUSE
YOU COMPLAINED ABOUT YOUR ATTENDANCE RATE, SO I'M COMING WITH YOU.
ALWAYS.
...JUST ALWAYS STICK WITH ME AT SCHOOL.

...AND NOW THIS ...
MOR-NING.
MOR-NING.
...IS HAPPENING.
Beverly Hills High School Diaries
Grr
erly Hills

...IS A BOTHER ...
...A WHITE SNAKE ...
BEFORE I KNEW IT ...
...I GOT IN TROUBLE AGAIN ...

I WON'T LET ANYONE TOUCH YOU.
IF A MERE SNAKE ...
...TAKES MY MASTER IN MARRIAGE ...
...MY NAME WILL SUFFER.
THAT'S ALL THIS IS ABOUT.
IN ANY CASE ...

...AND YOU RESCUED IT FROM BEING BULLIED ...
HMPH.
IT WAS A BEAUTIFUL WHITE SNAKE.
WELL, REJOICE.
THAT BEAUTIFUL SNAKE WILL COME TAKE YOU AWAY.
A beautiful...
...snake
...WILL COME TAKE ME AWAY ?!
A SNAKE MANAGED TO PUT THAT MARK ON YOU...
... BECAUSE YOU WEREN'T CAREFUL ENOUGH.
DON'T WORRY.
FLINCH

A MARK?
IT MEANS ...
...THAT YOU ARE NOW ENGAGED TO THAT SNAKE.
THIS IS THE MARK OF A SNAKE.
SO TELL ME HOW YOU BECAME BETROTHED TO A SNAKE ...
Pale
...AT SCHOOL.
A WHITE SNAKE WANDERED INTO SCHOOL ...

THIS MARK ON YOUR HAND.
WHERE'D YOU GET IT?
UH.
This ...
I TOUCHED A SNAKE AT SCHOOL ...
...THEN MY WRIST GOT SWOLLEN.
TOMOE?

Two

For this volume, I had Shun and Kaga-san draw a sidebar each. They always help out with my work. Wah, thanks! They drew Kurama and Nanami.

I really enjoy having other people draw my characters. Work is always a pleasure thanks to these two. Thank you!

Kaga-san can see the color of people's auras. When I have a chance, I ask, "What's my color now??" I ask thinking "I must be a calm pastel green now." Then I hear "vermilion" and feel gah.

The other day I asked, "What color is Chiro (the cat)?" and the result was "I can't tell because of the fur." Colors are interesting.

Shun can see the color of her own aura as well as other people's aura. The two both came up with the same color when I asked them. Wow. I cannot see auras. My eyesight is so poor, I cannot even see road signs. It would be fun if I could see more things.

TOMOE.
GRR
GRR
GRR
WHO ARE ...
...YOU FLIRTING WITH INSIDE THE SHRINE?
KSSSH
I DON'T BE-LIEVE THIS.
Chomp Chomp
YOU BROUGHT GIRLS TO THE SHRINE WHILE I WAS GONE.

THANKS FOR COMING, ASAGIRI AND YUGIRI.
I FEEL MUCH NEATER NOW.
YOU LOOK WONDER-FUL.
I'LL VISIT SOON.
MY, THAT'S WHAT YOU SAID LAST TIME.
BUT IT'S A SHAME.
I LOVED YOUR LONG HAIR TOO.
WHEN WILL YOU COME SEE US NEXT?

IS TOMOE AROUND ?
I WANT TO ASK HIM SOME-THING ...
TOMOE-DONO ...
...IS HAVING HIS HAIR CUT IN THE BACK GARDEN.
WELCOME HOME, NANAMI-SAMA.
WELCOME HOME!
HOW DO YOU LIKE IT, TOMOE-SAMA?

...IS ALL RED.
AS IF...
...A SNAKE WRAPPED AROUND AND BRUISED IT ...
Kssssh
I'M HOME.

Gah!
Momozono's touching it with her bare hands!
SLiTher
NOW.
DON'T COME WANDERING IN HERE ANYMORE.
IF THE SNAKE IS A KAMISAMA'S FAMILIAR, IT'S LIKE TOMOE.
TOMOE'S WHITE TOO...
HEY, MOMOZONO.
IS YOUR HAND ALL RIGHT...?
DON'T WORRY. IT DIDN'T BITE ME.
YOUR RIGHT HAND...

IT'S A WHITE SNAKE!
WHOA!
LET'S CATCH IT.
THWAK
THWAK
HEY.
TAP
WHITE SNAKES ARE SUPPOSED TO BE THE FAMILIARS OF KAMI-SAMA.
YOU'LL BE PUNISHED.

IT'S RAINING A LOT...

KSHHH

KYAH!

HEY, LOOK.

A SNAKE, A SNAKE!

Himeniko of the Swamp

Rules over the Tatara Swamp.

Owns lots of clothes.

Loves Kotaro.

Recently suffering from dry eyes.

Kamisama Kiss
Chapter 14

I'M FEELING WEIRD TODAY ...
OH DEAR.
...WASN'T SUPPOSED TO HAPPEN.
THIS...
REALLY! IT'S NOTHING!
SO JUST IGNORE ME.
IT'S NOTHING, ALL RIGHT ?!

WHAT IS IT? YOU GOT A STOMACH-ACHE?
IT'S BE-CAUSE YOU ...
YOU ...
...TOLD ME I'M BEAUTIFUL ...

I'M GLAD FOR YOU ...
...NANAMI.
SLAM
THANKS.
I WAS GETTING TIRED OF THOSE LITTLE ONES.
Tmp
Tmp
THE RYUGU PALACE IS A FRIGHT-ENING PLACE ...
NOW IS A GOOD TIME.
LET'S LEAVE, NANAMI.

I AM SO HONORED.
Nod Nod
WELL, PRIN-CESSES ...
... ENJOY THE MOONLIT NIGHT.
Sheesh! Go away!
Boo!

I DO NOT KNOW ANYBODY ...
...WHO'S MORE BEAUTIFUL THAN THIS KAMI.
Please ...
...let me escort you tonight.

POUT
WE ARE A HUNDRED TIMES MORE BEAUTIFUL THAN THIS HUMAN GIRL.
COME, COME.
WHAP
TOMOE-SAMA! WE WERE TALKING ABOUT SOMETHING IMPORTANT!
EXCUSE ME, PRIN-CESSES.
CHOOSE YOUR PARTNER FOR TONIGHT!
WHO'S THE MOST BEAUTI-FUL?

HIMEMIKO DRESSED ME UP.
HOW DO I LOOK ?
IF THE MAN YOU LOVE TELLS YOU HOW BEAUTIFUL YOU ARE ...
NANAMI.

HOW COULD SHE SELL ME TO THESE PRIN-CESSES ...?
I'M THE MOST BEAUTIFUL OF US THREE.
OH, HOW COULD YOU?
I'M THE MOST BEAUTI-FUL.
YOU YOUNG FISHES.
THIS IS WHY I HATE THE SWAMP GIRLS ...
QUIET DOWN.
I WILL NOT CONDONE ANY DISCOURTESIES TOWARD OUR GUESTS.

...ACTING STRANGE...
THAT IS THE MOONLIGHT ALGAE, TOMOE-SAMA.
THEY SHINE ONLY DURING A FULL MOON.
THIS IS BEAUTI-FUL.
I AM GLAD YOU SHOWED THEM TO ME.
PLEASE CHOOSE YOUR MATE FROM AMONG THE THREE OF US.
STAY IN THIS SWAMP FOR-EVER.
YES, YOU DO NOT NEED TO SERVE A HUMAN.
NANAMI ...
WHERE ARE YOU GOING ?!
WELL, NOW I SHALL—

IT IS MY TURN NOW.
YOU WILL FEEL LIKE RISING TO THE SKIES IF THE MAN YOU LOVE TELLS YOU HOW BEAUTIFUL YOU ARE.
I DON'T...
...LIKE TOMOE...
BUT I WONDER WHY...
...TODAY, I'M REALLY...

N—
A GIRL WANTS TO BE A FLOWER IN FRONT OF THE MAN SHE LOVES.
WHEN I WENT TO SEE KOTARO ...
...YOU DRESSED ME UP SO I LOOKED LOVELY.
...LIKE YOUR SHINSHI, DO YOU NOT?
I FELT VERY CONFIDENT ...
...EVEN THOUGH THAT WAS THE FIRST TIME I ENTERED THE HUMAN WORLD.

COME.
THIS IS ...
...MY DRESSING ROOM.
WHAAAA
GET READY TO DRESS HER UP.
YES.
NO!
I CAN'T BORROW SUCH EXPENSIVE-LOOKING KIMONOS!
I WON'T BE ABLE TO PAY FOR THEM IF I GET THEM DIRTY!
I DO NOT MIND.
YOU ...

NO! I'M NOT NERVOUS!
I CAME TO SEE YOU!
AND TOMOE ...
TOMOE WOULD RATHER BE WITH THOSE PRIN-CESSES.
THOSE CLOTHES.
YOU LENT ME THOSE ONCE.
COME NANAMI.
I SHALL LEND YOU A KIMONO.
WHA ...?

One

Hello.

I'm Julietta Suzuki. Thank you for reading vol. 3 of *Kamisama Kiss*! I'm happy if you enjoy reading it. ★

The other day, I went to Takachiho in Miyazaki Prefecture. This was a trip to relax (the main objective) with friends who were worn out from work. It was a good trip... I'd heard that a day would be enough to see everything, but it was impossible. We visited many shrines, and then the day was over.

There were many famous places mentioned in Japanese myths. The surroundings were beautiful. And the food was so, so delicious!

In Kyoto, you feel the history of humans, but in Takachiho, I felt the history of those not human. I was able to really relax and I'm full of energy again.

If you're thinking about traveling to Kyushu, please do go to Takachiho. I'd like to go visit again. I'd also like to go to Izumo (which I have been talking about with my editor) and Ise, which I haven't gone to yet. And Nikko. (I was able to go to Hakone. It was good).

There're no afterword pages in this volume, but please read the sidebars and extras.

See you.

THE WORLD TOMOE BELONGS TO.

I AM SORRY.

HIMEMIKO-SAMA. WE WOULD LIKE TO SHOW TOMOE-SAMA AROUND THE PALACE.
MAY WE TAKE HIM WITH US?
SURE.
YOU DO NOT MIND? NANAMI ...
WHAT ?
SURE.
I don't mind at all.
Take him, take him.

IT HAS BEEN A WHILE.
HOW MANY DECADES ...?
THE THREE YOUNG CARP PRINCESSES.
MY, MY ...
TODAY YOU'LL ESCORT ME.
OH NO, YOU'LL ESCORT ME.
AREN'T THEY, TOMOE-SAMA ?!
MY SCALES ARE MORE BEAUTIFUL.
WE HAVE GROWN UP TO BE BEAUTIFUL.
TOMOE-SAMA.
WE'RE NOT YOUNG CARP ANYMORE.
YES INDEED

...TOO PLAIN?
WAS THIS ...
Tug
N...
NO I'M N–
YOU MUST BE THINKING ...
...THAT YOU SHOULD'VE CHANGED.
Tomoe-sama.
SHING
LONG TIME NO SEE.
WE'VE BEEN WAITING FOR YOU!

...LET ME SHOW YOU THE WAY TO MY PALACE.
TONIGHT IS THE BRIGHTEST NIGHT BECAUSE OF THE MOONLIGHT.
I NEVER THOUGHT THE BOTTOM OF THE SWAMP WOULD BE SO BRIGHT ...
THIS IS BEAUTI-FUL ...
THAT'S THE NEW TOCHI-GAMI ...
Whisper
Whisper
OHO, SO THAT'S THE HUMAN TOCHI-GAMI ...
...

I HAVE PROMISED TO MEET KOTARO AGAIN ...
...SO I AM MAINTAINING SHINSHI-DONO'S TRANS-FORMATION SPELL INSIDE MY BODY.
...
...
HIME-MIKO, WHY DO YOU STILL LOOK LIKE A HUMAN?
WELL, LET US GO.
NOW NANAMI ...

IT HAS BEEN A WHILE ...
... NANAMI.
WAH!
I AM GLAD YOU LOOK FINE.
HIME-MIKO?
WAH!

I'M A FOOL.
MY HEART'S BEATING FAST.
AND I GOT MAD.
TODAY...
...I'M ACTING STRANGE.
SO ...
... WHERE'S HIME-MIKO?
I'M HERE.

YOU WOULDN'T WANT TO FALL IN LOVE WITH A FOX.
UH...
O-O-O-OF COURSE!
What're you saying ?!
SEE?
THAT'S WHAT I MEANT.

IF YOU FALL IN LOVE WITH A HUMAN GIRL ...
I WILL NOT FALL IN LOVE ...
...WITH A HUMAN WOMAN.

Fwoosh
TOMOE IS A FOX WITH NO TACT AT ALL.
ANYWAY, I'M LOOKING FORWARD TO SEEING HIMEMIKO.
HAVE SHE AND KOTARO GOTTEN CLOSER?
Fwoosh

Crnch
HOW CAN YOU SAY THAT?
Crnch
HOW CAN A CATFISH PRINCESS BECOME INTIMATE WITH A HUMAN?

TOMOE ...
GIRLS ARE DELICATE CREATURES.
DON'T SAY THAT KIND OF THING IN FRONT OF HER.

I'LL DRESS YOU.
What a beautiful full moon.
It's perfect for moon-gazing.
HER UNIFORM
WHY?
IT'S FINE!
THIS IS MY BEST FORMAL OUTFIT!

...YOU'RE ALREADY A FINE TOCHIGAMI.
JUST BE YOUR-SELF.
ALL RIGHT.
TOMOE-DONO, HOW ABOUT THIS FOR THE OBI?
NO, A PLAINER PATTERN ...
JUST BE MYSELF ...
UH, BUT I DON'T KNOW HOW TO WEAR A KIMONO.
DON'T WORRY.

WE'VE BEEN INVITED TO A TEA CEREMONY.
And this for the kosode.
HIME-MIKO'S MESSENGER CAME BY.
WH...
WHAT'RE YOU TALKING ABOUT?!
Gyah
YOU'LL WEAR THIS.
THEY WOULD LIKE THE TOCHIGAMI TO ATTEND...
...THE MOON-GAZING TEA PARTY BEING HELD TONIGHT AT HIMEMIKO'S PALACE.
ATTEND HIMEMIKO'S PARTY...
ME?
M...
EVEN IF YOU'RE JUST A LEVEL ONE...
WON'T I BE A NUI-SANCE?
MAY I REALLY GO?!

WELL, HE IS A FOX...
TOMOE-DONO.
I HAVE BROUGHT NANAMI-SAMA'S CLOTHES.
AH.
CALM DOWN, CALM DOWN ...
GOOD.
THIS ISN'T TOO FLASHY. YOU WON'T STAND OUT TOO MUCH.
IT'S A GOOD PATTERN.
WHA ...?
WHA ...?!

THINGS WEREN'T SUPPOSED TO BE THIS WAY...
I'M NOT BLUSHING!
BONK
YOU'RE BLUSH-
...BUT...
...MY HEART'S BEATING FAST...
YOU WANT SOME SOY SAUCE?
NO...
...AND THAT PISSES ME OFF A LITTLE.
WHAT?
...WHILE TOMOE ACTS THE SAME AS ALWAYS.

I RETURNED TO THE SHRINE TWO DAYS AGO.
GOOD MORNING, NANAMI.
SOME-THING WRONG?
I'VE BEEN ACTING WEIRD SINCE YESTERDAY.